How The Garden Grows

This book is dedicated
to

the dreamers,

the explorers,

And the adventurers
of tomorrow!

How The Garden Grows

by AmericKim Creations

Gardens are magical.

They are places that have been created to grow plants and flowers.

Plants and flowers grow from seeds.

Seeds hold the magical secrets of growing plants.

To create a garden we begin with planting seeds into the soil.

The seeds will need sunlight, food and water to grow.

The soil holds food for the seeds and keeps them safe.

Water helps the seeds grow big and strong.

Sunlight gives the seeds energy and keeps them warm.

The seeds grow,

and grow,

They grow until they sprout.

Then they grow some more.

And soon the sprout becomes a plant.

The plant keeps growing.

Some plants grow into flowers.

The flowers create pollen and nectar.

The pollen and nectar attract bees, butterflies and other insects

The insects feed on the pollen and nectar

The pollen stickes to the insects.

Pollen
Here

The insects spread the pollen
onto the next flowers they visit.

The pollen helps the flowers make more seeds.

When the garden plants have fully grown it will be time to harvest them.

Seeds can be collected from the harvested fruits, vegetables and flowers.

These seeds can be stored until time to plant again.

When it is almost time to plant your garden again, you can 'start' your stored seeds.

We call it "start" because we will help the seeds begin growing.

We 'start' seeds in a safe place, indoors until they have sprouted.

Once the seeds sprout, we plant them outside in the garden.

And our magical garden begins to grow again.

How the
Garden Grows

EAT YOUR VEGGIES

THE
END

www.ingramcontent.com/pod-product-compliance
Lightning Source LLC
Chambersburg PA
CBHW060900270326
41935CB00004B/55